THE MARKETING CAMPAIGN PLAYBOOK

A Step-by-Step Guide for Entrepreneurs, Marketers, and Small Business Owners

Sharon Lee Thony

Copyright © 2024 STK MKT Entertainment, LLC

All rights reserved

No part of this book may be reproduced, or stored in a retrieval system, or transmitted in any form or by any means, electronic, mechanical, photocopying, recording, or otherwise, without express written permission of the publisher.

CONTENTS

Title Page
Copyright
Dedication
Preface
Part 1: Understanding the Basics   1
Chapter 1: The Digital Marketing Landscape   3
Chapter 2: Setting Clear Objectives   9
Part 2: Crafting Compelling Campaigns   13
Chapter 3: Knowing Your Audience   15
Chapter 4: Content Creation and Strategy   23
Chapter 5: Social Media Marketing   32
Chapter 6: Search Engine Optimization (SEO)   37
Chapter 7: Email Marketing   41
Part 3: Executing and Managing Campaigns   47
Chapter 8: Planning and Execution   49
Chapter 9: Data-Driven Marketing   55
Chapter 10: Influencers and Partnerships   60
Part 4: Overcoming Challenges   63
Chapter 11: Managing Digital Marketing Budgets   65
Chapter 12: Adapting to Change   70
Chapter 13: Crisis and Reputation Management   74

Part 5: Real-World Success Stories	77
Chapter 14: Marketing that Worked (And Why)	79
Chapter 15: Insights from Industry Experts	84
Conclusion	91
Acknowledgement	93
About The Author	95

For Serge, Serge, and Solomon, who always inspire me to keep playing.

PREFACE

We've all been there.

Maybe you were at your desk, in a conference room, or sitting in front of a glowing ring light, staring into a Zoom call. Then comes the inevitable question, the one that makes you pause and think about your next move:

"So, where will your business (or brand) be in six months to a year?"

And then, more questions:

- How many customers do you have?
- What kind of growth do you expect in the next few years?
- Are you profitable?

If you're an entrepreneur, business owner, or marketer, you've likely faced these questions. They come at those key moments in your journey—moments when growth seems possible but figuring out how to get there feels tricky. Whether you're bootstrapping, taking out loans, or raising capital, there's one thing that remains at the heart of it all: your customers.

Getting and keeping customers takes a solid marketing plan, but building campaigns that consistently deliver can feel overwhelming. The tools, strategies, and channels are always changing, and it's easy to get lost in the noise. That's exactly why I created this playbook.

The Marketing Campaign Playbook is your step-by-step guide to making sense of it all. After more than 20 years of working with global brands and growing my own digital marketing agency, I've learned what really works when it comes to marketing that drives results. This book is packed with those proven strategies and practical steps, designed to help you create campaigns that convert and grow your business.

Think of it as your go-to playbook—a resource that breaks down every stage of building successful marketing campaigns, from setting goals to executing with confidence. Whether you're just starting out or scaling up, this playbook gives you the clarity and tools you need to keep moving forward.

Because marketing isn't just about getting your name out there—it's about creating something that lasts, something that grows with you and your business.

PART 1: UNDERSTANDING THE BASICS

SHARON LEE THONY

CHAPTER 1: THE DIGITAL MARKETING LANDSCAPE

The digital marketing landscape has undergone a rapid evolution over the past decade, driven by advances in technology, changes in consumer behavior, and the growth of online platforms. For small business owners and entrepreneurs, understanding this dynamic environment is crucial to successfully navigate the world of digital marketing and leverage it to grow their businesses.

Overview of the Current Digital Marketing Environment

Digital marketing has become a critical component of any business strategy. Today, consumers expect brands to have a robust online presence, and businesses of all sizes must engage their target audiences across multiple digital channels to stay competitive. The shift from traditional advertising (like print and TV) to digital platforms has leveled the playing field, allowing small businesses to compete with larger brands by reaching specific audiences with targeted messages.

The current digital marketing environment is defined by a few key characteristics:

- **Data-Driven Decision Making**: Marketers now have access to vast amounts of data that allow them to make informed decisions about their campaigns. Tools like Google Analytics and Facebook Insights help businesses track user behavior, campaign performance, and ROI in real time.

- **Personalization and Customer Experience**: Consumers increasingly expect personalized experiences. Businesses that can deliver tailored content, recommendations, and interactions are more likely to build long-term relationships with their customers.
- **Mobile-First Focus**: With mobile devices being the primary way people access the internet, businesses must ensure that their digital presence—whether it be websites, apps, or social media—is optimized for mobile use.

These factors have shaped the strategies businesses use to reach their audiences, making it essential for small businesses to adapt to these new norms.

Key Digital Marketing Channels and Their Significance

1. **Social Media Marketing**
   - **Significance**: Social media platforms like Facebook, Instagram, LinkedIn, and Twitter have become vital tools for businesses to engage with their audience. Social media allows for direct communication with customers, brand building, and the promotion of products and services through organic posts and paid ads.
   - **Best Practices**: Small businesses can use social media to build community, share valuable content, and run targeted ad campaigns that are cost-effective and highly customizable. Instagram and TikTok, for example, are powerful for visual storytelling and influencer marketing, while LinkedIn is key for B2B networking and thought leadership.

2. **Search Engine Optimization (SEO)**
   - **Significance**: SEO is the process of optimizing a website to rank higher on search engine results pages (SERPs). Given that Google processes over 3.5 billion searches per day, being discoverable via search engines

is essential for driving organic traffic to a business's website.
- **Best Practices**: Small businesses should focus on both on-page (e.g., keywords, meta descriptions) and off-page SEO (e.g., backlinks) to improve their search rankings. Local SEO is also crucial for businesses that rely on geographic proximity, as it helps them appear in local search results.

3. **Content Marketing**
   - **Significance**: Content marketing involves creating valuable, relevant content (such as blog posts, videos, and infographics) to attract and engage a target audience. Unlike traditional advertising, content marketing focuses on providing information that solves problems and builds trust with potential customers.
   - **Best Practices**: Small businesses can use content marketing to establish themselves as industry experts, improve SEO, and nurture customer relationships through consistent, high-quality content.

4. **Email Marketing**
   - **Significance**: Despite the rise of social media, email marketing remains one of the most effective channels for reaching customers directly. It offers a high ROI and allows businesses to send personalized messages, promotions, and updates directly to their subscribers.
   - **Best Practices**: Building and segmenting an email list, crafting compelling subject lines, and creating engaging content are key to successful email campaigns. Automation tools can help businesses streamline their email marketing efforts and deliver timely messages to their audience.

5. **Pay-Per-Click Advertising (PPC)**
   o **Significance**: PPC advertising, such as Google Ads, allows businesses to place ads on search engines and pay only when users click on them. This can be an effective way for small businesses to drive traffic and conversions quickly, especially for those with limited SEO visibility.
   o **Best Practices**: Small businesses should focus on targeting the right keywords, optimizing landing pages, and setting a clear budget to ensure their PPC campaigns are effective and cost-efficient.

Trends and Emerging Technologies in Digital Marketing

1. **Artificial Intelligence and Machine Learning**
   o AI and machine learning are revolutionizing digital marketing by enabling more personalized and automated campaigns. Tools like chatbots, predictive analytics, and programmatic advertising are becoming essential components of modern marketing strategies. AI-driven tools can also help small businesses automate customer service, analyze data, and optimize campaigns more efficiently.

2. **Video and Live Streaming**
   o Video content continues to dominate digital marketing. Platforms like YouTube, TikTok, and Instagram Live provide businesses with opportunities to connect with their audience in a more engaging and authentic way. Live streaming, in particular, allows for real-time interaction with customers, fostering a sense of community and immediacy.

3. **Voice Search Optimization**
   o With the growing popularity of smart speakers and voice assistants like Alexa and Siri, voice search is becoming a significant trend. Businesses need to

optimize their content for voice search by focusing on conversational keywords and providing direct answers to common questions.

4. **Influencer Marketing**
    o Influencer marketing has proven to be an effective way for small businesses to reach new audiences. By partnering with influencers who align with their brand values, businesses can leverage the influencer's credibility and reach to promote their products or services.

5. **Augmented Reality (AR) and Virtual Reality (VR)**
    o AR and VR technologies are emerging as powerful tools for immersive marketing experiences. From virtual try-ons to interactive product demos, these technologies allow businesses to engage customers in new and innovative ways, making them particularly valuable for e-commerce and retail.

6. **Sustainability and Social Responsibility**
    o Consumers are increasingly concerned with environmental and social issues, and they expect brands to align with their values. Businesses that embrace sustainability, ethical practices, and social responsibility in their marketing efforts are more likely to build loyalty and trust with their audience.

Key Takeaway:

The digital marketing landscape is constantly evolving, but the opportunities for small businesses and entrepreneurs have never been greater. By staying informed about the latest trends and utilizing the right channels, businesses can build powerful marketing campaigns that drive growth and success.

CHAPTER 2: SETTING CLEAR OBJECTIVES

Success in digital marketing, especially for small businesses and entrepreneurs, begins with a clear understanding of your goals. Setting objectives that align with your business vision is essential to ensuring that your marketing efforts are purposeful, measurable, and ultimately, effective. In this chapter, we'll explore the importance of setting SMART goals, discuss how to align marketing objectives with broader business goals, and provide examples of effective goal-setting for small businesses.

Importance of Setting SMART Goals

SMART goals are a powerful tool in digital marketing. The SMART framework ensures that your goals are:

- **Specific**: Clearly define what you want to achieve. Ambiguous goals like "increase sales" are difficult to act on. Instead, be precise, such as "increase online sales by 15% over the next quarter."
- **Measurable**: Ensure that your goals can be quantified. This means attaching a number or metric to your objective, such as the percentage increase in website traffic or a specific number of new email subscribers.
- **Achievable**: Your goals should be realistic and attainable. Setting overly ambitious goals can be demotivating, whereas achievable goals provide a sense of progress and accomplishment. For example, doubling your customer base in a year might be feasible for a small business, but tripling it

could be unrealistic.
- **Relevant**: Align your goals with your overall business objectives. Each marketing goal should contribute to your broader vision and strategy. For instance, if your business goal is to expand into a new market, your marketing objectives should focus on building brand awareness in that area.
- **Time-bound**: Set a clear timeframe for achieving your goals. This helps create urgency and provides a deadline for assessing your progress. For example, "Increase social media followers by 20% in the next six months" gives your team a specific timeframe to work within.

By setting SMART goals, you create a roadmap that guides your digital marketing efforts and provides a framework for evaluating your success.

Aligning Marketing Objectives with Overall Business Goals

Aligning your marketing objectives with your overall business goals ensures that your digital marketing efforts directly contribute to the growth and success of your business. Marketing objectives should never exist in a vacuum; they must support your broader business strategy. Here's how to achieve this alignment:

1. **Identify Your Business Objectives**: Start by identifying your business's primary objectives, such as increasing revenue, expanding your customer base, or entering new markets. These goals will serve as the foundation for your marketing strategy.
2. **Translate Business Goals into Marketing Objectives**: Once you've identified your business objectives, translate them into actionable marketing goals. For example, if your business goal is to increase revenue by 20% in the next year, your marketing objective might be to generate a 25% increase in qualified leads through targeted digital campaigns.
3. **Ensure Consistency Across Channels**: Your marketing

objectives should be consistent across all digital channels. If your goal is to build brand awareness, for instance, make sure your social media strategy, content marketing efforts, and email campaigns are all working towards that same objective.
4. **Monitor and Adjust**: Regularly monitor your progress towards both your marketing and business goals. If your marketing efforts aren't delivering the desired results, be ready to adjust your strategy. This flexibility ensures that your marketing objectives remain aligned with your evolving business needs.

Examples of Effective Goal-Setting for Small Businesses

To illustrate how SMART goals and alignment with business objectives can be applied in real-world scenarios, here are a few examples:

1. **Increasing Brand Awareness**:
   - **Business Goal**: Build brand recognition in a new geographic market.
   - **Marketing Objective**: Increase brand mentions on social media by 30% over the next six months through influencer partnerships and targeted social media ads.
   - **SMART Breakdown**: The goal is specific (increase brand mentions), measurable (by 30%), achievable (by leveraging influencer partnerships and ads), relevant (supports the business's expansion goal), and time-bound (within six months).

2. **Driving Website Traffic**:
   - **Business Goal**: Boost online sales by 15% in the next quarter.
   - **Marketing Objective**: Increase website traffic by 25% through a combination of SEO improvements, content

marketing, and pay-per-click (PPC) advertising.
- **SMART Breakdown**: The goal is specific (increase website traffic), measurable (by 25%), achievable (through SEO, content marketing, and PPC), relevant (supports the business's goal of boosting online sales), and time-bound (within the next quarter).

3. **Growing an Email Subscriber List**:
- **Business Goal**: Launch a new product line and drive sales through email marketing.
- **Marketing Objective**: Increase the email subscriber list by 40% over the next three months by offering exclusive content and discounts to new subscribers.
- **SMART Breakdown**: The goal is specific (grow the email list), measurable (by 40%), achievable (through content and discount offers), relevant (supports the product launch strategy), and time-bound (within three months).

These examples demonstrate how small businesses can set clear, actionable marketing objectives that align with their broader business goals. By doing so, they create a cohesive strategy that drives measurable results and supports long-term growth.

Key Takeaway:

Setting clear objectives is the foundation of any successful digital marketing strategy. By using the SMART framework and ensuring alignment with your business goals, you can create focused, actionable marketing plans that contribute to your company's overall success.

PART 2: CRAFTING COMPELLING CAMPAIGNS

SHARON LEE THONY

CHAPTER 3: KNOWING YOUR AUDIENCE

In digital marketing, the most successful campaigns are those that resonate deeply with the intended audience. Understanding who your customers are, what they need, and how they behave is crucial for crafting marketing strategies that truly connect. This chapter will guide you through the process of identifying and understanding your target audience, conducting market research, creating buyer personas, and using audience insights to tailor your marketing strategies.

Identifying and Understanding Your Target Audience

Your target audience is the specific group of people most likely to be interested in your product or service. Identifying this group is the first step in creating a focused marketing strategy. For small businesses and entrepreneurs, understanding your audience means recognizing their demographics, psychographics, behaviors, and needs. Here's how to identify your target audience:

1. **Start with Your Product or Service**:
   - Consider what problem your product or service solves. Who is most likely to experience this problem, and who would benefit the most from your solution?
   - Think about the unique value your product or service offers and who is most likely to appreciate it.

2. **Analyze Your Current Customer Base**:
   - If you already have customers, study their demographics,

behaviors, and preferences. What do they have in common? Who are your most loyal customers?
- Collect data from sales records, customer feedback, and social media analytics to identify patterns in your audience.

3. **Research Your Competition**:
- Look at the target audience of your competitors. Who are they marketing to, and how are they positioning their products?
- Analyzing your competition can provide valuable insights into potential market segments that you may have overlooked.

4. **Segment Your Audience**:
- Audience segmentation involves dividing your broad target audience into smaller groups based on characteristics like age, gender, location, income, interests, or behavior.
- Segmenting your audience allows you to tailor your marketing messages to each group more effectively. For example, a fitness business might have different messaging for young professionals interested in high-intensity workouts and older adults focused on wellness and mobility.

Conducting Market Research and Creating Buyer Personas

Once you have a general idea of who your audience is, conducting market research will help you gain deeper insights into their behaviors, needs, and preferences. Market research can be conducted through surveys, focus groups, interviews, and online analytics tools. Here's how to conduct effective market research:

1. **Use Surveys and Polls**:
- Surveys are a cost-effective way to gather data directly from your audience. You can ask questions

about their preferences, challenges, and habits.
- Tools like Google Forms, SurveyMonkey, or even social media polls can help you collect valuable feedback from your target market.

2. **Analyze Social Media and Website Data**:
- Social media platforms like Facebook, Instagram, and LinkedIn provide robust analytics tools that offer insights into your audience's demographics, behaviors, and engagement patterns.
- Google Analytics is another essential tool for understanding how users interact with your website, which pages are most popular, and where your traffic comes from.

3. **Conduct Customer Interviews and Focus Groups**:
- For more in-depth insights, conduct interviews or focus groups with existing or potential customers. These discussions can reveal pain points, desires, and motivations that quantitative data might not capture.

With the data you've gathered, you can create detailed **buyer personas**—fictional representations of your ideal customers. Buyer personas help you humanize your audience and keep their needs at the forefront of your marketing efforts. Here's how to create effective buyer personas:

1. **Define Key Demographics**:
- Start by outlining the basic demographics of your persona, including age, gender, location, occupation, income level, and education. For example, "Sarah, a 35-year-old marketing manager living in New York City."

2. **Understand Their Goals and Challenges**:
- What are your persona's primary goals? What challenges do they face that your product or service can help solve? For instance, Sarah might be looking for effective tools

to streamline her team's digital marketing efforts.

3. **Map Out Their Behavior**:
   - Consider how your persona interacts with brands online. Do they prefer email newsletters, social media, or video content? What factors influence their purchasing decisions? This information helps you determine which channels and messaging will be most effective in reaching them.

4. **Give Them a Story**:
   - Bring your persona to life by giving them a brief backstory that summarizes their needs, challenges, and goals. For example, "Sarah is a busy marketing manager who's always on the lookout for new tools and strategies to help her team improve their digital campaigns. She values efficiency and appreciates brands that offer personalized support."

Creating multiple personas that represent different segments of your audience allows you to tailor your marketing strategies to meet the specific needs of each group.

Using Audience Insights to Tailor Your Marketing Strategies

Once you've identified your target audience and developed buyer personas, it's time to use these insights to inform your marketing strategies. Tailoring your marketing efforts to your audience ensures that your messages resonate with the right people at the right time. Here's how to do it:

1. **Personalize Your Messaging**:
   - Use the information from your buyer personas to create personalized marketing messages. For example, if one segment of your audience values sustainability, highlight your brand's eco-friendly practices in your communications.
   - Personalization extends beyond just the content of

your messaging—it also includes how and where you deliver it. Some personas might respond better to email marketing, while others prefer engaging with brands on social media.

2. **Select the Right Channels**:
- Different audience segments prefer different platforms. Use your audience insights to determine which digital channels are most effective for reaching each persona.
- For example, if one of your personas spends most of their time on Instagram, prioritize that platform for visually-driven content. Alternatively, if another persona prefers long-form content, focus on blog posts, white papers, and email newsletters.

3. **Segment Your Campaigns**:
- Audience segmentation allows you to run more targeted campaigns. Instead of sending a one-size-fits-all message to your entire audience, tailor your campaigns to address the specific needs of each segment.
- For example, if you run a fitness business, you might create separate campaigns for weight loss, strength training, and wellness, each targeting different audience segments with content and offers that are relevant to their interests.

4. **Continuously Optimize Based on Feedback**:
- Digital marketing allows for real-time feedback and optimization. Use the data from your campaigns to monitor performance and make adjustments as needed.
- Pay attention to metrics like click-through rates, conversion rates, and customer engagement to determine whether your strategies are resonating with your target audience. If not, use this data to refine your approach.

Buyer Persona Example: Emily Davis – The Health-Conscious Millennial

A business targeting this persona, Emily Davis, would likely be in the health and wellness industry. The business would need to emphasize transparency, quality, and alignment with Emily's values of health and sustainability to effectively connect with her.

Name: Emily Davis

Age: 29

Gender: Female

Location: Seattle, WA

Occupation: Marketing Coordinator at a Health and Wellness Company

Education: Bachelor's Degree in Communications

Background:

Emily is a marketing professional who is passionate about living a healthy lifestyle. She enjoys yoga, cooking nutritious meals, and is always on the lookout for the latest health trends. Emily lives in a bustling urban area with access to a variety of fitness centers and organic food stores.

Goals and Aspirations:

- **Personal Goals:** To maintain a balanced, healthy lifestyle while managing a demanding career.
- **Professional Goals:** To advance in her career by contributing innovative marketing strategies that align with her values of health and sustainability.

Challenges:

- **Time Management:** Balancing a busy work schedule with her personal health goals.
- **Information Overload:** Navigating the overwhelming amount of health information and products available online.

Interests and Hobbies:

- Practicing yoga and meditation
- Experimenting with new, healthy recipes
- Attending wellness workshops and seminars

Values:

- Health and wellness
- Sustainability and eco-friendliness
- Authenticity and transparency in brands

Buying Behavior:

- **Decision-Making Process:** Emily values in-depth research before making purchases. She prefers brands that provide detailed information about their products and align with her values of health and sustainability.
- **Preferred Channels:** She frequently shops online and follows health and wellness influencers on social media for recommendations.

Pain Points:

- **Quality Assurance:** Difficulty finding reliable products that truly meet health and sustainability claims.
- **Price Sensitivity:** Struggles to find high-quality, eco-friendly products that fit her budget.

Marketing Message:

"To Emily, health is not just a trend but a lifestyle. She seeks brands that offer authentic, high-quality products that align with her values. By highlighting product benefits, providing transparent information, and emphasizing sustainability, you can connect with Emily on a deeper level."

Example Campaign Idea:

- **Campaign Name:** "Elevate Your Wellness Journey"
- **Description:** A content series featuring behind-the-scenes looks at how products are made, emphasizing their health benefits and eco-friendly practices. Include testimonials from health experts and influencers who resonate with Emily's values. Utilize social media ads and influencer partnerships to reach her effectively.

Key Takeaway:

Knowing your audience is the key to unlocking the full potential of your digital marketing efforts. By identifying and understanding who your customers are, conducting thorough market research, and creating detailed buyer personas, you can tailor your marketing strategies to connect with your audience in meaningful and impactful ways. This knowledge empowers you to build campaigns that resonate, drive engagement, and ultimately, contribute to your business's success.

CHAPTER 4: CONTENT CREATION AND STRATEGY

Content is at the heart of every successful digital marketing campaign. It's how you communicate your brand's story, engage your audience, and drive them to take action. However, creating compelling content requires more than just producing random pieces of content—it demands a well-thought-out strategy that aligns with your brand and resonates with your audience. In this chapter, we'll explore how to develop an effective content strategy, the types of content that resonate with audiences, and best practices for content creation and distribution.

Developing a Content Strategy That Aligns with Your Brand

A content strategy is a comprehensive plan that outlines how your business will use content to achieve its marketing objectives. It serves as a roadmap for creating, publishing, and managing content that supports your brand's goals. Here's how to develop a content strategy that aligns with your brand:

1. **Define Your Brand's Message and Voice**:
   - Start by clearly defining your brand's message. What do you want your audience to know about your brand? What values and mission does your brand stand for?
   - Your brand voice should reflect your message and resonate with your target audience. For example, a playful and informal tone might work for a lifestyle

brand targeting millennials, while a more authoritative tone might be appropriate for a B2B tech company.

2. **Set Clear Goals**:
   - Your content strategy should be driven by specific marketing goals, whether it's increasing brand awareness, generating leads, or driving conversions. Each piece of content should have a clear purpose that aligns with these goals.
   - For instance, if your goal is to increase website traffic, your content strategy might focus on creating SEO-optimized blog posts that rank highly on search engines.

3. **Understand Your Audience**:
   - Use the insights gained from Chapter 3 to tailor your content to your audience's needs, preferences, and behaviors. Your content should address their pain points, answer their questions, and provide value.
   - Consider creating different types of content for different segments of your audience. For example, a blog post that educates beginners on your industry might appeal to new customers, while an in-depth white paper might resonate with more experienced professionals.

4. **Plan Your Content Types and Topics**:
   - Identify the types of content that align with your goals and resonate with your audience (more on this below). Then, brainstorm content topics that are relevant, timely, and engaging.
   - Create a content calendar that outlines when and where you'll publish each piece of content. This ensures that your content strategy is consistent and aligns with your marketing campaigns.

5. **Measure and Optimize**:
   o Once you've launched your content, track its performance using metrics like engagement, shares, conversions, and SEO rankings. Regularly review these metrics to understand what's working and what needs improvement.
   o Based on these insights, optimize your content strategy to better meet your goals. This could involve tweaking your content topics, experimenting with different formats, or adjusting your distribution channels.

Types of Content That Resonate with Audiences

Different types of content resonate with audiences in different ways. By offering a variety of content formats, you can engage your audience more effectively and cater to their diverse preferences. Here are some key types of content that tend to perform well across digital channels:

1. **Blog Posts**:
   o **Why They Resonate**: Blogs are a versatile content format that allows you to share valuable information, showcase your expertise, and improve your website's SEO. They're great for educating your audience on topics relevant to your industry and driving traffic to your site.
   o **Best Practices**: Focus on creating long-form, high-quality blog posts that address your audience's pain points. Use keyword research to optimize your posts for search engines, and promote your blogs on social media to increase visibility.

2. **Videos**:
   o **Why They Resonate**: Video content is one of the most engaging formats available. It's dynamic, visual, and can convey complex information in a simple, easy-to-

digest way. Videos are especially effective on platforms like YouTube, Instagram, and TikTok.
- **Best Practices**: Keep your videos concise, visually appealing, and aligned with your brand's voice. Include a clear call to action and optimize your videos for mobile viewing. Consider live streaming as a way to engage your audience in real-time.

3. **Infographics**:
- **Why They Resonate**: Infographics are powerful tools for presenting data and complex information in a visually appealing and easily digestible format. They're highly shareable on social media, making them great for increasing brand visibility.
- **Best Practices**: Focus on clarity and simplicity in your design. Use infographics to highlight key statistics, steps in a process, or comparisons. Make sure your infographics align with your brand's visual identity and include a clear call to action.

4. **Podcasts**:
- **Why They Resonate**: Podcasts allow brands to connect with audiences on a more personal level. They're ideal for storytelling, interviews, and in-depth discussions, and they appeal to people who prefer consuming content on the go.
- **Best Practices**: Focus on producing high-quality audio and providing valuable insights or entertainment. Consistency is key—regularly release new episodes and promote them across your digital channels.

5. **Ebooks and White Papers**:
- **Why They Resonate**: Ebooks and white papers are excellent for in-depth, authoritative content that showcases your expertise and provides valuable insights. They're often used as lead magnets,

encouraging users to exchange their contact information for access.
- **Best Practices**: Make sure your ebooks and white papers are well-researched, professionally designed, and aligned with your audience's needs. Use them to dive deep into topics that require more than a blog post or infographic can cover.

6. **Social Media Posts**:
- **Why They Resonate**: Social media platforms are essential for engaging with your audience, building brand awareness, and driving traffic to your website. Social media posts can include everything from images and videos to polls and stories.
- **Best Practices**: Tailor your content to each platform's unique format and audience. For example, Instagram thrives on high-quality visuals, while LinkedIn is ideal for thought leadership content. Be consistent with your posting schedule and engage with your followers by responding to comments and messages.

Best Practices for Content Creation and Distribution

Creating great content is only half the battle—distributing it effectively is just as important. Here are some best practices for content creation and distribution:

1. **Consistency is Key**:
- Regularly producing and publishing content keeps your brand top-of-mind for your audience. Stick to a content calendar to ensure you're consistently delivering value to your followers.

2. **Optimize for SEO**:
- SEO (Search Engine Optimization) is critical for ensuring your content is discoverable by search engines. Use keyword research to identify terms your

audience is searching for, and optimize your content's titles, headers, and meta descriptions accordingly.

3. **Repurpose Content:**
   - Maximize the value of your content by repurposing it in different formats. For example, you can turn a blog post into an infographic, a podcast episode, or a series of social media posts. This allows you to reach different segments of your audience while saving time and resources.

4. **Leverage Multiple Channels:**
   - Distribute your content across various digital channels to maximize its reach. Promote your blog posts on social media, send your latest video to your email subscribers, and use paid advertising to amplify high-performing content.
   - Each platform has its own strengths, so tailor your content for each channel while ensuring consistency in your brand messaging.

5. **Engage with Your Audience:**
   - Content creation isn't a one-way street — engage with your audience by responding to comments, encouraging feedback, and starting conversations. This fosters a sense of community and builds stronger relationships with your customers.

6. **Analyze and Optimize:**
   - Continuously track your content's performance using analytics tools. Look at metrics such as page views, social shares, engagement rates, and conversion rates to evaluate how well your content is performing.
   - Use this data to refine your content strategy, focusing on what's working and making adjustments to improve

underperforming content.

Example: Content Strategy for XYZ Skincare

Background: XYZ Skincare, a boutique skincare brand, aimed to boost online visibility and sales by enhancing their content strategy. They focused on leveraging specific tactics to create impactful content.

Objective: Increase brand awareness and drive conversions through a strategic content approach.

Content Creation Strategy:
The Step-by-Step Approach

1. Audience Analysis

Tools Used: Google Analytics, Facebook Insights

Findings: The target audience consists of environmentally conscious millennials interested in natural beauty products.

2. Content Themes and Topics:

Theme 1: Eco-Friendly Beauty
    Topic: "5 Sustainable Ingredients You'll Love"
    Format: Blog post with detailed analysis and infographics
Theme 2: Behind-the-Scenes
    Topic: "How We Create Our Best-Selling Facial Oil"
    Format: Instagram Stories and YouTube video
Theme 3: Customer Testimonials
    Topic: "Real Stories: How Our Customers Achieved Glowing Skin"
    Format: Facebook posts and Twitter threads

3. Content Formats and Channels:

Blog Posts: Use SEO tools like Ahrefs to identify high-traffic keywords related to skincare. Post bi-weekly, optimized for SEO.

Social Media Posts:
    Frequency: Daily posts on Instagram and Facebook
    Content Types: Product showcases, behind-the-scenes videos, and user-generated content
    Tools: Canva for design, Later for scheduling

Email Newsletters:
    Frequency: Monthly
    Content: Include a roundup of blog posts, exclusive offers, and new product announcements
    Tools: Mailchimp for email campaigns

4. Content Calendar:

Setup: Use a tool like Google Sheets or Trello to plan content

Implementation: Schedule blog posts for Mondays, social media updates for daily posts, and newsletters for the first Monday of each month.

5. Engagement and Optimization:

Engagement: Respond to comments within 24 hours, use A/B testing for email subject lines

Optimization: Track performance using Google Analytics and social media insights; adjust strategy based on engagement metrics and conversion rates

Results:

- **Website Traffic:** 35% increase in organic traffic to blog posts
- **Social Media Engagement:** 50% increase in engagement rate, with higher interaction on posts featuring user-generated

content
- **Sales Conversion:** 20% increase in conversion rates from social media campaigns due to targeted call-to-action (CTA) placements

---

Key Takeaway:

Content creation and strategy are essential elements of a successful digital marketing campaign. By developing a well-defined content strategy that aligns with your brand, producing content that resonates with your audience, and following best practices for content creation and distribution, you can create compelling campaigns that drive engagement, build brand loyalty, and contribute to your business's growth.

CHAPTER 5: SOCIAL MEDIA MARKETING

Social media is a powerful tool that enables businesses of all sizes to connect with their audience, build brand awareness, and drive engagement. However, achieving success on social media requires more than just posting regularly—it involves choosing the right platforms, creating engaging content, and strategically utilizing social media advertising. In this chapter, we'll explore how to choose the right social media platforms for your business, create shareable content, and leverage social media advertising to boost your reach and engagement.

Choosing the Right Social Media Platforms for Your Business

With so many social media platforms available, it can be tempting to try to establish a presence on all of them. However, spreading yourself too thin can dilute your efforts. Instead, focus on the platforms that are most relevant to your business and where your target audience spends their time. Here's how to choose the right platforms:

1. **Identify Your Target Audience**:
    - Refer back to your buyer personas to understand which platforms your audience is using. For example, if your target market includes Gen Z, you might focus on platforms like TikTok or Instagram, while LinkedIn might be better suited for B2B companies targeting professionals.

2. **Consider Your Content**:
   o Different platforms favor different types of content. If your business produces a lot of visual content, Instagram and Pinterest might be the right fit. For video content, YouTube and TikTok are excellent platforms. If you focus on long-form content and thought leadership, LinkedIn and Medium could be effective channels.

3. **Analyze Competitors**:
   o Look at where your competitors are most active and successful. This can give you an idea of where your audience is most likely to engage with similar brands.

4. **Evaluate Resources and Time**:
   o Consider your team's capacity and resources. It's better to focus on a few platforms and do them well than to spread yourself too thin across too many channels.

Creating Engaging and Shareable Content

To stand out on social media, your content must be engaging, relevant, and shareable. Here are some strategies to create content that resonates with your audience:

1. **Know Your Audience's Preferences**:
   o Use insights from social media analytics to understand what types of content your audience engages with the most. Do they prefer short videos, informative infographics, or behind-the-scenes content?

2. **Tell Stories**:
   o Storytelling is a powerful tool for creating emotional connections with your audience. Share stories about your brand, your team, or your customers. Authenticity and transparency often lead to higher engagement.

3. **Use High-Quality Visuals**:
   - Visual content tends to perform better on social media. Invest in high-quality images, videos, and graphics to make your content stand out. Make sure your visuals are consistent with your brand's aesthetic.

4. **Encourage Interaction**:
   - Ask questions, create polls, and encourage your audience to share their thoughts in the comments. The more interaction your posts generate, the more likely they are to be seen by a wider audience.

5. **Incorporate User-Generated Content (UGC)**:
   - User-generated content, such as customer reviews, testimonials, and photos, can be incredibly powerful. Sharing UGC not only builds trust with your audience but also encourages others to engage with your brand.

Utilizing Social Media Advertising to Boost Reach and Engagement

While organic social media strategies are essential, social media advertising can amplify your reach and help you achieve specific goals more quickly. Here's how to effectively use social media ads:

1. **Define Your Advertising Goals**:
   - Start by identifying your goals. Are you looking to increase brand awareness, drive traffic to your website, generate leads, or boost sales? Your goals will determine the type of ad campaigns you run and the platforms you use.

2. **Target the Right Audience**:
   - Social media platforms offer powerful targeting options

based on demographics, interests, behaviors, and more. Use these targeting features to reach the right audience with your ads. Retargeting ads, which focus on people who have already interacted with your brand, can also be highly effective.

3. **Test Different Ad Formats**:
o   Experiment with various ad formats, such as image ads, video ads, carousel ads, and stories ads, to see which ones resonate best with your audience. Different formats work better for different goals—video ads, for example, are often more effective for driving engagement, while carousel ads can showcase multiple products.

4. **Monitor and Optimize**:
o   Track the performance of your ads using metrics like click-through rates, conversion rates, and return on ad spend (ROAS). Use this data to optimize your campaigns, adjusting your targeting, ad copy, or budget to improve results.

Key Takeaway

Social media marketing is a powerful tool for building brand awareness, engaging with your audience, and driving conversions. To succeed, it's essential to understand the platforms your audience frequents and tailor your content to fit the style and preferences of each. Creating authentic, shareable content that resonates with your audience, along with leveraging the unique strengths of different platforms—such as Instagram's visual storytelling, LinkedIn's professional networking, or TikTok's short-form videos—can lead to significant growth. Remember that consistency, engagement, and data-driven strategies are key to optimizing your social media campaigns. Tracking metrics like reach, engagement, and conversion rates helps refine your approach and ensure you're maximizing the impact of your efforts across all channels.

CHAPTER 6: SEARCH ENGINE OPTIMIZATION (SEO)

Search engine optimization (SEO) is a critical component of any digital marketing strategy. By optimizing your website and content for search engines, you can improve your visibility, drive organic traffic, and ultimately, increase conversions. In this chapter, we'll cover the basics of SEO, key on-page and off-page SEO techniques, and tools and resources to help you improve your website's search ranking.

Basics of SEO and Why It's Crucial for Your Business

SEO is the practice of optimizing your website to rank higher on search engine results pages (SERPs) for relevant keywords. Higher rankings mean more visibility, which can lead to increased traffic and sales. Here's why SEO is crucial for your business:

1. **Organic Search is a Primary Source of Traffic**:
   - Organic search (unpaid search results) is often the largest source of traffic for websites. By ranking highly for relevant keywords, you can attract more visitors to your site without relying solely on paid advertising.
2. **SEO Builds Trust and Credibility**:
   - Ranking well in search results can enhance your brand's credibility. Users tend to trust websites that appear on the first page of search results, viewing them as more authoritative and reliable.

3. **SEO Provides Long-Term Results**:
   o   Unlike paid advertising, which stops delivering results as soon as you stop paying, SEO can provide long-term benefits. Once your website ranks well for key terms, it can continue to attract traffic over time with minimal ongoing effort.

On-Page and Off-Page SEO Techniques

To improve your website's search ranking, you need to implement both on-page and off-page SEO techniques. Here's how:

1. **On-Page SEO**:

   o   **Keyword Research**: Start by conducting keyword research to identify the terms and phrases your target audience is searching for. Use tools like Google Keyword Planner, SEMrush, or Ahrefs to find relevant keywords with good search volume and low competition.
   o   **Optimize Content**: Incorporate your target keywords into your website's content, including titles, headers, meta descriptions, and body text. However, avoid keyword stuffing—your content should be natural and valuable to readers.
   o   **Improve Site Structure**: Make sure your site is easy to navigate, with a clear hierarchy and internal linking structure. Use descriptive, keyword-rich URLs and ensure your site is mobile-friendly.
   o   **Enhance Page Speed**: Page speed is a ranking factor in Google's algorithm, so optimizing your site for fast load times is crucial. Compress images, leverage browser caching, and use a content delivery network (CDN) to improve speed.

2. **Off-Page SEO**:

- **Backlink Building**: Backlinks, or links from other websites to yours, are one of the most important off-page SEO factors. Focus on building high-quality backlinks from reputable sites in your industry. Guest blogging, influencer outreach, and creating shareable content are all effective strategies for earning backlinks.
- **Social Signals**: Although not a direct ranking factor, social signals (likes, shares, and comments on social media) can indirectly influence your SEO. Content that gets shared widely on social media is more likely to attract backlinks, which can improve your search rankings.
- **Local SEO**: If you're a local business, optimizing for local search is crucial. Claim and optimize your Google My Business listing, encourage customer reviews, and ensure your business's name, address, and phone number (NAP) are consistent across the web.

Tools and Resources to Improve Your Website's Search Ranking

A variety of tools and resources can help you improve your SEO efforts. Here are some of the most popular ones:

1. **Google Analytics and Google Search Console**:
   - Google Analytics provides valuable insights into your website's traffic and performance, while Google Search Console allows you to monitor your site's presence in Google search results. Both tools are essential for tracking your SEO progress.

2. **SEMrush and Ahrefs**:
   - These comprehensive SEO tools offer features for keyword research, backlink analysis, site audits, and competitor analysis. They're invaluable for identifying opportunities to improve your search rankings.

3. **Yoast SEO (WordPress Plugin):**
    - If you're using WordPress, the Yoast SEO plugin can help you optimize your content for search engines. It provides real-time suggestions for improving your on-page SEO, such as keyword usage, meta descriptions, and readability.

4. **Moz:**
    - Moz offers a suite of SEO tools, including a keyword explorer, link building tools, and site audits. Moz also provides helpful resources and guides for learning more about SEO best practices.

Key Takeaway

Effective SEO involves optimizing your website and content to improve visibility on search engines and attract the right audience. It's not just ranking high on search results, but delivering valuable content that aligns with what your target customers are searching for. By leveraging keyword research, on-page optimization, and building credible backlinks, you can enhance your site's authority and drive organic traffic, ultimately boosting your business growth. SEO is a long-term strategy that requires consistency and adaptability as search algorithms evolve.

CHAPTER 7: EMAIL MARKETING

Email marketing remains one of the most effective digital marketing channels for building relationships with customers, driving conversions, and nurturing leads. In this chapter, we'll discuss how to build and segment your email list, craft compelling email campaigns, and measure the success of your email marketing efforts.

Building and Segmenting Your Email List

Your email list is one of your most valuable marketing assets. Building and segmenting your list allows you to send targeted messages that resonate with different groups within your audience. Here's how to do it effectively:

1. **Building Your Email List**:

    - **Lead Magnets**: Offer valuable resources such as ebooks, checklists, or exclusive discounts in exchange for email addresses.

    - **Subscription Forms**: Place subscription forms in high-traffic areas of your website, such as the homepage, blog posts, and landing pages. Make it easy for users to subscribe by keeping the form simple and straightforward.
    - **Social Media**: Use social media to promote your email newsletter and encourage followers to subscribe.

2. **Segmenting Your Email List:**

    o **Demographics**: Segment your list based on key demographic information such as age, location, or gender. This allows you to tailor your messages to the specific needs and interests of different groups.

    o **Behavioral Data**: Segment your audience based on their behavior, such as previous purchases, website activity, or email engagement. For example, you might send different messages to customers who have abandoned their shopping carts versus those who have made recent purchases.

    o **Engagement Levels**: Create segments based on how engaged your subscribers are with your emails. You can target highly engaged subscribers with loyalty offers, while re-engagement campaigns can be sent to those who haven't interacted in a while.

Crafting Compelling Email Campaigns

Once you have a segmented list, the next step is to craft compelling email campaigns that drive results. Here are some best practices for creating effective email marketing campaigns:

1. **Personalization:**
    o Personalization goes beyond just addressing the recipient by name. Use data from your segmentation to deliver personalized content that speaks directly to your audience's needs and interests.

2. **Strong Subject Lines:**
    o The subject line is the first thing recipients see, and it determines whether they'll open your email. Make your subject lines clear, concise, and compelling. Use

curiosity, urgency, or exclusivity to encourage opens.

3. **Engaging Content**:
   - Your email content should be engaging and relevant to your audience. Use a mix of text, images, and calls-to-action (CTAs) to create a visually appealing email that captures attention. Be sure to keep your content concise and focused, with a clear message.

4. **Mobile Optimization**:
   - With a large percentage of emails being opened on mobile devices, it's crucial to ensure your emails are mobile-friendly. Use responsive design, keep your text readable, and make sure your CTAs are easy to tap on small screens.

5. **Testing and Optimization**:
   - Continuously test different elements of your emails, such as subject lines, content, and CTAs, to see what resonates best with your audience. Use A/B testing to optimize your campaigns for better results.

Measuring Email Marketing Success and Optimizing for Better Results

To ensure your email marketing campaigns are effective, it's essential to measure their performance and make data-driven decisions to optimize future efforts. Here are some key metrics to track:

1. **Open Rates**:
   - Open rates indicate how many recipients opened your email. A low open rate might suggest that your subject lines need improvement, or that your audience isn't engaged.

2. **Click-Through Rates (CTR)**:

- CTR measures how many recipients clicked on a link within your email. This metric can help you gauge how effective your content and CTAs are at driving action.

3. **Conversion Rates**:
- Conversion rates track how many recipients completed the desired action after clicking through your email, such as making a purchase or filling out a form. This is a key indicator of your email campaign's effectiveness.

4. **Bounce Rates**:
- Bounce rates show how many of your emails were undeliverable. A high bounce rate could indicate issues with your email list, such as outdated or invalid email addresses.

5. **Unsubscribe Rates**:
- Unsubscribe rates reveal how many recipients opted out of your email list after receiving your email. If your unsubscribe rate is high, it may be a sign that your content isn't resonating with your audience or that you're sending emails too frequently.

6. **Revenue Per Email**:
- For e-commerce businesses, tracking the revenue generated per email can provide insights into the direct financial impact of your email marketing efforts.

By regularly analyzing these metrics, you can identify what's working and what's not, allowing you to make informed adjustments to your email marketing strategy.

Example: GreenGlow's Email Marketing Strategy

GreenGlow, a small e-commerce business specializing in eco-friendly skincare products, seeks to promote its new range of organic facial oils while strengthening relationships with existing customers.

1. Segmentation

To tailor its communication, GreenGlow divides its email list into three key segments:

- **Previous customers** who have already purchased from the brand.
- **New subscribers** who have not yet made a purchase.
- **High-value customers** who have made multiple purchases in the past.

2. Personalization

GreenGlow customizes its emails for each segment:

- For **previous customers**, the email references the last product they bought and offers a personalized discount on the new facial oils.
- **New subscribers** receive an educational email explaining the benefits of organic skincare and are invited to try a free sample with their first purchase.
- **High-value customers** receive an exclusive invitation to a pre-sale event, giving them early access to the new product line with a special discount.

3. Content Creation

Each email is designed with visually appealing images of the new facial oils, customer testimonials, and a clear, compelling call-to-action (CTA). The CTA varies by segment, with phrases like "Shop Now and Get 20% Off" or "Try Our New Facial Oils Today" to encourage immediate engagement.

4. A/B Testing

To optimize results, GreenGlow runs A/B tests on:

- **Subject lines**, comparing "Introducing Our New Organic Facial Oils" vs. "A Special Offer Just for You."
- **CTAs**, testing the effectiveness of "Shop Now" vs. "Try it Today."

5. Results

By applying segmentation, personalization, and A/B testing, GreenGlow achieves significant improvements in its email marketing campaign:

- **Open rates** increase to 25%, up from the usual 15%.
- **Click-through rates** for the exclusive pre-sale offer reach 7%, driving a 12% increase in sales from high-value customers.

Through these strategies, GreenGlow successfully engages its audience, enhances customer loyalty, and generates higher sales from its latest product launch.

Key Takeaway

Email marketing remains one of the most effective digital marketing channels for building relationships, nurturing leads, and driving conversions. To succeed, it's essential to focus on delivering value to your audience through personalized, segmented content. Consistent testing, optimizing subject lines, calls-to-action (CTAs), and design will help improve open rates, click-through rates (CTR), and overall campaign performance.

PART 3: EXECUTING AND MANAGING CAMPAIGNS

CHAPTER 8: PLANNING AND EXECUTION

Executing a successful digital marketing campaign requires meticulous planning and efficient execution. This chapter covers the essential steps to plan and execute a campaign, including setting timelines, budgets, and KPIs, with real-world examples of successful campaigns.

Steps to Plan and Execute a Digital Marketing Campaign

1. **Define Campaign Objectives:**
   - Start by clearly defining what you want to achieve. Whether it's increasing brand awareness, driving sales, or generating leads, your objectives will guide every decision throughout the campaign.

2. **Identify Your Target Audience:**
   - Understanding who you're targeting is crucial. Develop detailed buyer personas that represent your ideal customers, and tailor your messaging and channels accordingly.

3. **Develop a Content Strategy:**
   - Your content strategy should align with your objectives and audience. Decide on the types of content (e.g., blogs, videos, social media posts) that will resonate most and plan how you will distribute it across different channels.

4. **Set Timelines and Budgets:**

- Create a detailed timeline for each phase of the campaign, from content creation to launch to follow-up. Set a budget that covers all aspects, including content production, advertising spend, and tools for tracking performance.

5. **Establish Key Performance Indicators (KPIs):**
   - Determine the metrics that will help you measure the success of your campaign. KPIs might include click-through rates, conversion rates, social media engagement, or return on investment (ROI).

6. **Execute the Campaign:**
   - Launch your campaign according to the plan, ensuring that all team members are aligned and that the necessary resources are in place. Monitor the campaign closely to make real-time adjustments as needed.

Real-World Examples of Successful Campaign Planning

Dove's "Real Beauty" Campaign

Overview: Dove's "Real Beauty" campaign aimed to redefine beauty standards by challenging societal norms and celebrating women of all shapes, sizes, and colors. The campaign was launched in 2004 and has since become a hallmark of brand storytelling and emotional marketing.

Insight: A successful campaign requires an in-depth understanding of the audience and a message that resonates emotionally. This campaign demonstrated the power of aligning marketing objectives with a culturally relevant and empowering message.

Planning Tools and Resources:

1. **Market Research & Audience Insights:**

   Dove began by conducting extensive research that revealed a staggering insight: only 2% of women considered themselves beautiful. This data drove the campaign's messaging and reinforced Dove's mission to redefine beauty.

2. **Clear Objectives:**

   Dove's primary objective was to increase brand affinity by addressing the gap between societal beauty ideals and how women perceive themselves. This goal guided all content and communication strategies.

3. **Content Strategy:**

   Dove created emotionally driven content, including videos, social media posts, and print ads, showcasing real women rather than traditional models. The use of authentic storytelling resonated with their audience on a deep, personal level.

4. **Media Planning & Distribution:**

   The campaign was distributed across multiple channels, including TV commercials, social media, print, and out-of-home advertising. Dove leveraged traditional and digital media for maximum reach and engagement, ensuring that the campaign would spark conversation in both public spaces and online communities.

5. **Collaborations & Partnerships:**

   Dove partnered with advocacy groups and influencers to amplify the message of the campaign, making it part of a larger cultural conversation about self-esteem and beauty standards. This helped reinforce the brand's authenticity and commitment to social issues.

Results:

Dove's "Real Beauty" campaign significantly boosted brand awareness and loyalty. Sales for Dove products increased from $2.5 billion to $4 billion within the campaign's first decade, while also establishing the brand as a champion of body positivity.

Airbnb's "We Accept" Campaign

Overview: Launched in response to growing social and political tension around immigration and inclusivity, Airbnb's "We Accept" campaign reaffirmed the company's commitment to belonging and acceptance for all. The campaign featured a powerful video ad during the 2017 Super Bowl and was part of a broader effort to align the brand with social justice.

Insight: Strategic campaign planning allows a brand to take a stand on social issues, aligning its message with its core values while creating a powerful, relevant narrative.

Planning Tools and Resources:

1. **Audience Analysis & Cultural Insight**:

   Airbnb understood that its users were global, open-minded, and socially aware. Through research and data, they identified that a message of inclusivity would resonate deeply with their core audience and reflect their values of belonging.
2. **Messaging & Brand Positioning**:

   The campaign's core message, "We Accept," reinforced Airbnb's positioning as a global brand that welcomes all, regardless of background. The messaging was rooted in a strong belief system that not only addressed political tension but also highlighted Airbnb's role in creating a global community.

3. **Video as the Hero Asset**:

   Airbnb created a compelling 30-second video ad featuring diverse faces with the powerful message of acceptance and inclusion. The emotional impact of this video was heightened by its placement during the Super Bowl, one of the most widely viewed events in the world.

4. **Multi-Channel Distribution**:

   While the video ad was the centerpiece, the campaign extended beyond TV. Airbnb launched supporting digital and social media campaigns that encouraged users to share their own stories of acceptance, thus generating user-generated content. Additionally, Airbnb revamped its website to highlight initiatives supporting refugees and those affected by the immigration crisis.

5. **Community Engagement & Social Responsibility**:

   Airbnb backed up their message with action. They pledged to provide short-term housing for 100,000 displaced individuals and refugees, showing their commitment to making a tangible difference. This initiative was integrated into the campaign, which helped enhance their credibility and reinforce brand loyalty.

Results:

The campaign received widespread acclaim and was shared across social media platforms, with millions of views and shares. Airbnb also saw a significant increase in bookings and brand engagement. Most importantly, the campaign strengthened Airbnb's position as a brand that stands for inclusivity and acceptance, resonating deeply with its global community of users.

Fun Fact: I had the incredible opportunity to work on Dove's iconic "Real Beauty" campaign early in my career. It was a transformative experience that showed me the power of thoughtful, purpose-driven marketing. This campaign remains one of my personal favorites!

Key Takeaway

Successful campaign planning is rooted in setting clear objectives, understanding your audience, and strategically using the right tools to execute a cohesive marketing strategy. By integrating market research, cross-channel distribution, and measurable goals, businesses can create campaigns that resonate with their target audience and drive meaningful results. Thoughtful planning and execution ensure that marketing efforts are both impactful and scalable.

CHAPTER 9: DATA-DRIVEN MARKETING

In today's digital landscape, data is a vital component of any marketing strategy. This chapter delves into the importance of data in digital marketing, the tools available for tracking and analyzing performance, and how to use data insights to refine and improve your campaigns.

Importance of Data in Digital Marketing

1. **Informed Decision-Making:**
   o   Data allows marketers to make informed decisions based on actual user behavior and trends rather than assumptions. This leads to more effective and targeted campaigns.

2. **Personalization:**
   o   With the right data, you can personalize content and offers to match the specific needs and preferences of your audience, increasing engagement and conversion rates.

3. **Optimizing Campaign Performance:**
   o   By continuously monitoring data, you can identify what's working and what isn't, allowing for real-time adjustments that can optimize performance and improve ROI.

Tools for Tracking and Analyzing Campaign Performance

1. **Google Analytics**:
   - A powerful tool for tracking website traffic, user behavior, and conversion rates. Google Analytics provides detailed insights into how users interact with your site and where they drop off.

2. **HubSpot**:
   - An all-in-one marketing platform that offers tools for managing campaigns, tracking leads, and analyzing performance. HubSpot's dashboards provide real-time data on key metrics.

3. **Hootsuite**:
   - For social media campaigns, Hootsuite offers robust analytics that track engagement, reach, and audience demographics across multiple platforms.

Using Data Insights to Refine and Improve Campaigns

1. **A/B Testing**:
   - Use A/B testing to compare different versions of your content or ads. This helps you determine which version performs better, enabling you to optimize your campaigns for maximum effectiveness.

2. **Segmentation**:
   - Segment your audience based on data insights, such as demographics or past behavior. This allows for more targeted and relevant marketing efforts.

3. **Continuous Improvement**:
   - Regularly review your data and campaign performance

to identify areas for improvement. Use these insights to refine your strategy and achieve better results over time.

Example: Data-Driven Marketing for FreshFlare

Background: FreshFlare, an e-commerce brand offering organic skincare products, needed to improve their marketing strategy to increase conversions and optimize their return on ad spend. They adopted a data-driven approach to better understand the performance of their marketing efforts.

Objective: Boost conversion rates and reduce customer acquisition costs by leveraging data insights to optimize marketing channels and campaign strategies.

Audience Analysis:

- **Tools Used:** Google Analytics, Instagram Insights, Klaviyo for email tracking
- **Findings:** The core audience consists of environmentally conscious women, ages 25-40, who are frequent users of Instagram and value personalized shopping experiences.

Key Data Insights and Tactics:

- **Insight 1:** Instagram ads had high engagement but low conversion rates.
    - **Tactic:** Implement retargeting campaigns focused on users who abandoned their carts.
    - **Format:** Carousel ads featuring personalized offers.
- **Insight 2:** Email marketing had high conversion rates but low reach.
    - **Tactic:** Increase email list size through targeted

lead-generation ads on Instagram and Facebook.
- **Format:** Pop-up forms on website and social media ads offering discounts for sign-ups.
- **Insight 3:** Website visitors often dropped off at the product description page.
  - **Tactic:** Optimize product pages with user reviews and product recommendation widgets to keep visitors engaged.
  - **Format:** Updated website design using Hotjar to analyze visitor behavior.

Content Formats and Channels:

- **Instagram Ads:**
  - **Type:** Carousel ads with personalized messaging
  - **Tools:** Facebook Ads Manager for targeting, Canva for ad design
  - **Frequency:** Weekly ad campaigns targeting cart abandoners
- **Email Marketing:**
  - **Type:** Segmented email campaigns based on customer behavior
  - **Tools:** Klaviyo for segmentation and automation
  - **Frequency:** Bi-weekly, focusing on abandoned cart reminders and exclusive offers
- **Website Optimization:**
  - **Type:** Improved product pages with user-generated content and recommendations
  - **Tools:** Hotjar for tracking user behavior, Shopify for website updates
  - **Frequency:** Ongoing A/B testing to refine product page layout

Engagement and Optimization:

- **Engagement:** Respond to Instagram comments and messages

within 24 hours, use A/B testing for ad creatives and email subject lines
- **Optimization:** Continuously track campaign performance using Google Analytics and Klaviyo, adjusting based on engagement and conversion data.

Results:

- **Conversion Rate:** 20% increase in conversion rates from retargeted Instagram ads
- **Email Performance:** 25% increase in email sign-ups and a 30% boost in sales from email marketing
- **Customer Acquisition Cost (CAC):** 15% reduction in CAC due to more efficient targeting and optimization of high-performing channels

---

Key Takeaway

Data-driven marketing is essential for creating campaigns that perform and scale. By analyzing customer behaviors, market trends, and campaign metrics, businesses can make informed decisions that optimize their strategies in real-time. Data enables marketers to allocate resources efficiently, focus on the tactics that yield the best results, and continually refine their approach. When used effectively, data empowers brands to drive measurable growth and create more personalized, impactful marketing efforts.

CHAPTER 10: INFLUENCERS AND PARTNERSHIPS

Influencers and strategic partnerships can significantly amplify the reach and impact of your digital marketing campaigns. This chapter explores how to identify and collaborate with influencers, build strategic partnerships, and provides case studies of successful campaigns.

Identifying and Collaborating with Influencers in Your Industry

1. **Choosing the Right Influencers**:
   - Look for influencers who align with your brand values and have a genuine connection with their audience. Their followers should overlap with your target audience.

2. **Building Relationships**:
   - Approach influencers with a genuine interest in their work. Build a relationship based on mutual respect and trust before discussing collaboration opportunities.

3. **Creating Authentic Campaigns**:
   - Work with influencers to create content that feels authentic and resonates with their audience. Authenticity is key to maintaining credibility and trust.

Building Strategic Partnerships to Expand Your Reach

1. **Identifying Potential Partners**:
   - Look for businesses or organizations that complement your brand and share your target audience. Strategic partnerships can help you reach new customers and add value to your offerings.

2. **Negotiating Partnerships**:
   - Clearly define the goals, roles, and expectations for both parties. Ensure that the partnership benefits both sides and aligns with your overall marketing strategy.

3. **Co-Marketing Campaigns**:
   - Develop co-marketing campaigns that leverage the strengths of both partners. This could include joint content creation, shared promotions, or collaborative events.

Case Studies of Successful Influencer and Partnership Campaigns

1. **Daniel Wellington's Influencer Strategy**:
   - The watch brand Daniel Wellington used a wide network of micro-influencers to grow its brand. By leveraging influencers with small but highly engaged followings, they created a buzz and significantly increased sales.

2. **GoPro and Red Bull's Partnership**:
   - GoPro and Red Bull partnered on content creation, events, and promotions that aligned with both brands' focus on extreme sports and adventure. The partnership boosted visibility and reinforced their brand identities.

Key Takeaway

Leveraging influencers and strategic partnerships is a powerful way to expand a brand's reach, build credibility, and drive results. Effective influencer marketing goes beyond follower counts, focusing on finding individuals who genuinely connect with your target audience and align with your brand's values. Partnerships, whether through collaborations or formal alliances, should be built on mutual objectives and clearly defined outcomes. By thoughtfully integrating these elements into your campaigns, you can create authentic, impactful connections that enhance your brand's overall marketing efforts.

PART 4: OVERCOMING CHALLENGES

CHAPTER 11: MANAGING DIGITAL MARKETING BUDGETS

Managing a digital marketing budget effectively is crucial, especially for small businesses with limited resources. This chapter will guide readers through the process of allocating their marketing budget wisely, explore cost-effective strategies, and provide case studies of successful budget management.

Allocating Your Marketing Budget Effectively

1. **Understanding Your Business Goals**:
   - Begin by aligning your budget with your business goals. Determine what you want to achieve—whether it's brand awareness, lead generation, or customer retention—and allocate funds accordingly.

2. **Prioritizing High-Impact Channels**:
   - Focus on the marketing channels that offer the best return on investment (ROI) for your business. For small businesses, this might include social media, email marketing, and search engine optimization (SEO).

3. **Tracking and Adjusting**:
   - Continuously monitor your spending and campaign performance. Be prepared to reallocate funds to the channels that are delivering the best results.

Cost-Effective Marketing Strategies for Small Businesses

1. **Content Marketing**:
   - Invest in creating high-quality content that educates and engages your audience. Blogging, video marketing, and infographics are cost-effective ways to build brand awareness and drive traffic.

2. **Social Media Marketing**:
   - Leverage the power of social media platforms to connect with your audience. Organic posts, community engagement, and targeted ads on platforms like Facebook and Instagram can be very effective.

3. **Email Marketing**:
   - Build and nurture your email list with personalized campaigns. Email marketing is one of the most cost-effective channels, offering a high ROI when done correctly.

Case Studies of Successful Budget Management

Dollar Shave Club: Maximizing Impact with a Minimal Budget

Dollar Shave Club's success is a classic example of how a small budget, when allocated strategically, can yield massive results. The brand's viral video, produced for just $4,500, reached millions and established Dollar Shave Club as a disruptor in the razor industry.

Key Budget Management Strategies:

- **Content Creation with a Focus on Virality:** Rather than investing in expensive production, Dollar Shave Club focused on creating content that resonated with their audience. The humorous and straightforward messaging made the video highly shareable, reducing the need for paid promotion.
- **Leveraging Owned and Earned Media:** They relied heavily on their website and social media platforms to distribute the video, minimizing distribution costs. The campaign went viral organically, generating significant earned media value without additional ad spend.
- **Investing in Direct-to-Consumer Channels:** By focusing on a subscription model, Dollar Shave Club minimized costs associated with retail distribution, using the initial marketing success to build a direct relationship with their customers. The low-budget marketing efforts were crucial in enabling this direct-to-consumer approach, which sustained long-term growth.

This case illustrates the power of prioritizing creativity and customer engagement over high production budgets.

Airbnb: Scaling Without Heavy Ad Spend

Airbnb's early marketing efforts focused on building a community around shared experiences rather than spending heavily on traditional advertising. This allowed them to scale globally on a relatively lean marketing budget, relying on innovative budget management strategies.

Key Budget Management Strategies:

- **Content Marketing and Storytelling:** Airbnb capitalized on user-generated content, encouraging hosts and guests to share their stories. By turning their users into brand ambassadors, they created a wealth of engaging content at minimal cost.

This also built trust and credibility, helping Airbnb compete with established hotel chains.
- **Harnessing the Power of Social Media:** Social media platforms, particularly Instagram and Facebook, became key distribution channels for Airbnb's content. Rather than investing heavily in paid advertising, Airbnb focused on organic growth and word-of-mouth referrals.
- **Grassroots Marketing and Partnerships:** In the early days, Airbnb forged partnerships with events such as SXSW, offering free housing to attendees. This helped build brand awareness without substantial ad spend, using experiential marketing to engage a targeted, influential audience.

By concentrating their efforts on content creation, user engagement, and grassroots marketing, Airbnb managed to grow its brand exponentially while keeping marketing costs under control.

Key Takeaway

Effective budget management is about more than just cutting costs—it's about strategically allocating resources to maximize impact. By focusing on high-return activities like content creation, organic growth, and leveraging low-cost channels, brands like Dollar Shave Club and Airbnb were able to achieve significant results without heavy financial investment. Success lies in prioritizing channels and tactics that drive measurable outcomes, constantly reviewing performance, and being flexible enough to adapt when necessary. Proper budget management is key to sustaining growth and maintaining profitability in the long term.

CHAPTER 12: ADAPTING TO CHANGE

The digital marketing landscape is constantly evolving, with new trends and technologies emerging at a rapid pace. This chapter discusses the importance of staying agile, adapting strategies to new trends, and provides examples of businesses that successfully navigated change.

Staying Agile in a Rapidly Changing Digital Landscape

1. **Embracing a Growth Mindset**:
   - Encourage a culture of continuous learning within your team. Stay curious and open to new ideas, and be willing to experiment with different strategies.

2. **Regularly Reviewing and Updating Strategies**:
   - Regularly assess your marketing strategies to ensure they remain relevant. This includes keeping an eye on industry trends, customer behavior, and technological advancements.

3. **Leveraging Data and Analytics**:
   - Use data and analytics to inform your decisions. This will help you identify trends early and adjust your strategies in real-time.

Adapting Your Strategies to New Trends and Technologies

1. **Adopting Emerging Technologies:**
   - Stay ahead of the curve by adopting new technologies, such as artificial intelligence (AI), chatbots, and automation tools. These can streamline your marketing efforts and improve customer experiences.

2. **Exploring New Channels:**
   - As new social media platforms and digital channels emerge, consider testing them out to reach new audiences. However, ensure that these channels align with your brand and target audience.

3. **Flexibility in Content Formats:**
   - Be flexible with your content formats. For example, the rise of short-form video content on platforms like TikTok and Instagram Reels has opened up new opportunities for brands to engage with audiences in creative ways.

Real-Life Examples of Businesses That Successfully Adapted to Change

Netflix: From DVD Rentals to Streaming Giant Netflix originally began as a DVD rental service but saw the potential of streaming as the digital landscape evolved. By embracing change and transitioning its business model, Netflix became a leader in the entertainment industry, revolutionizing how people consume media.

Key Adaptation Strategies:

- **Pivot to Streaming:** Recognizing early on that broadband

internet could support streaming, Netflix shifted from physical DVDs to digital content delivery. This allowed them to meet changing consumer demands for instant, on-demand entertainment.
- **Personalization through Data:** Netflix used customer data to offer personalized recommendations, improving user experience and increasing engagement.
- **Investment in Original Content:** By moving into content creation, Netflix not only attracted more subscribers but also differentiated itself from competitors with exclusive, original programming.
- **Continuous Evolution:** Netflix's adaptability, from DVD rentals to streaming and then to content creation, demonstrates their ability to evolve with market changes and technological advancements.

By adapting quickly to technological shifts, Netflix successfully positioned itself as a global leader in entertainment, proving the value of agility and foresight in business strategy.

Lush Cosmetics: Prioritizing Direct Customer Relationships
Lush Cosmetics took a bold stance by leaving social media in 2021, focusing on building direct relationships with customers through owned channels. This decision allowed Lush to stay true to their brand values and foster more meaningful customer interactions.

Key Adaptation Strategies:

- **Exit from Social Media:** Citing concerns over mental health and data privacy, Lush stepped away from platforms like Instagram and Facebook, differentiating itself in a market where most brands were investing more in social media.
- **Focus on Owned Channels:** Lush redirected efforts to email marketing, website content, and in-store experiences to create stronger, more personal customer connections.

- **Brand Alignment:** By prioritizing its ethical stance on mental health and privacy, Lush reinforced its reputation as a brand committed to its values, which resonated with its loyal customer base.

By prioritizing direct engagement and ethical principles, Lush adapted to changes in the digital landscape while staying aligned with their core mission, ultimately strengthening their brand identity.

Key Takeaway

Adaptability is crucial for long-term business success, as shown by companies like Netflix and Lush Cosmetics. Netflix's evolution from DVD rentals to a streaming giant and content creator demonstrates the power of foresight and willingness to embrace technological change. Lush Cosmetics, on the other hand, highlights the importance of staying true to brand values, even when it means taking bold steps like leaving social media. Both companies show that adapting to change—whether through technology or customer engagement—can lead to sustained growth and success in a competitive market.

CHAPTER 13: CRISIS AND REPUTATION MANAGEMENT

In the digital age, managing your online reputation and handling crises effectively is more important than ever. This chapter offers strategies for managing your brand's reputation, responding to negative feedback, and handling crises, with examples of successful crisis management.

Strategies for Managing Your Online Reputation

1. **Proactive Reputation Management**:
   - Regularly monitor your brand's online presence, including social media mentions, reviews, and news articles. Use tools like Google Alerts and social listening platforms to stay informed.

2. **Engaging with Your Audience**:
   - Actively engage with your audience online, responding to both positive and negative feedback. Transparency and authenticity are key to building and maintaining trust.

3. **Encouraging Positive Reviews**:
   - Encourage satisfied customers to leave positive reviews on platforms like Google, Yelp, and industry-specific sites. Positive reviews can help counterbalance any

negative feedback.

Responding to Negative Feedback and Handling Crises

1. **Addressing Negative Feedback**:
   o Respond to negative feedback promptly and professionally. Acknowledge the issue, apologize if necessary, and offer a solution. Turning a negative experience into a positive one can enhance your brand's reputation.

2. **Developing a Crisis Management Plan**:
   o Have a crisis management plan in place that outlines how to handle different types of crises, from product recalls to social media blunders. This plan should include designated spokespeople, communication channels, and a step-by-step action plan.

3. **Effective Communication During a Crisis**:
   o During a crisis, clear and timely communication is crucial. Keep your audience informed with regular updates, and be transparent about the steps you're taking to resolve the issue.

Examples of Effective Crisis Management

Tylenol's Response to the 1982 Cyanide Crisis: In 1982, Johnson & Johnson faced a devastating crisis when several people in Chicago died after taking Tylenol capsules laced with cyanide. This incident could have destroyed the Tylenol brand, but the company's swift and transparent response turned it into a textbook example of effective crisis management. Johnson & Johnson immediately ordered a nationwide recall of Tylenol, pulling over 31 million bottles from shelves at a cost of over $100 million. They halted production and advertising to focus entirely on consumer safety. Additionally, the company introduced tamper-proof packaging, a move that set new industry standards for product safety. Tylenol's quick, transparent communication and prioritization of public trust over short-term profits helped restore its reputation and consumer confidence.

Starbucks' Response to the Philadelphia Incident: In 2018, Starbucks found itself at the center of a public relations crisis after two black men were arrested at a Philadelphia store for trespassing while waiting for a friend. The incident sparked national outrage, with accusations of racial profiling aimed at the company. Starbucks' leadership quickly acknowledged the severity of the situation and took decisive action. They closed over 8,000 stores nationwide for a day to conduct racial bias training for employees. Starbucks also reviewed and updated its company policies, ensuring that everyone could use their stores as public spaces, regardless of making a purchase. This proactive approach to addressing racial bias and the company's transparency in admitting fault helped mitigate the damage to their brand, showing a commitment to learning from mistakes and making systemic changes.

Key Takeaway

Effective crisis management is essential for protecting a brand's reputation during unforeseen challenges. Companies must respond swiftly and transparently to maintain public trust, prioritizing customer safety and open communication. A well-prepared crisis plan can help mitigate damage, while learning from mistakes strengthens long-term brand loyalty. By addressing issues head-on and taking responsibility, businesses can not only recover but emerge stronger, setting new standards in their industry.

PART 5: REAL-WORLD SUCCESS STORIES

SHARON LEE THONY

◆ ◆ ◆

CHAPTER 14: MARKETING THAT WORKED (AND WHY)

In this chapter, we examine some of the most successful digital marketing campaigns that have earned recognition for their innovation and impact. These case studies provide a detailed breakdown of each campaign, highlighting the strategies that led to their success, the lessons learned, and key takeaways that small businesses can apply to their own marketing efforts.

Successful Digital Marketing Campaigns

1. **The ALS Ice Bucket Challenge**:
   - **Overview**: A viral social media campaign that raised over $115 million for ALS research in the summer of 2014.
   - **Strategy**: Leveraged user-generated content, social sharing, and a clear call-to-action.
   - **Key Takeaways**: Demonstrated the power of viral marketing and social media engagement. The simplicity and shareability of the campaign were key to its success.

2. **Nike's "Just Do It" Campaign**:
   - **Overview**: A long-standing campaign that has continually evolved to resonate with new generations, focusing on motivational messaging and social issues.

- **Strategy**: Integrated storytelling with influencer marketing and a strong brand identity.
- **Key Takeaways**: Showcased the importance of brand consistency and the ability to adapt to cultural trends. Nike's use of high-profile athletes and influencers helped amplify the message.

3. **Old Spice's "The Man Your Man Could Smell Like"**:
- **Overview**: A humorous and memorable campaign that revitalized the Old Spice brand.
- **Strategy**: Focused on creative, humorous content and an interactive digital presence, including a series of personalized video responses.
- **Key Takeaways**: Highlighted the importance of creativity and engagement in marketing. The campaign's viral success was driven by its unique and entertaining approach.

Lessons Learned and Key Takeaways from Each Campaign

- **Viral Potential**: Simplicity, relatability, and a strong call-to-action can propel a campaign to viral status.

- **Storytelling**: Authentic and compelling storytelling connects with audiences on a deeper level and enhances brand loyalty.

- **Adaptability**: Successful campaigns often adapt to cultural trends and audience preferences, keeping the brand relevant and engaging.

How Small Businesses Can Replicate These Strategies

- **Leverage Social Media**: Use social media platforms to create shareable and engaging content that resonates with your target audience.

- **Focus on Storytelling**: Develop a narrative that aligns with your brand's values and speaks directly to your audience's needs and desires.

- **Engage Your Audience**: Encourage user participation through challenges, contests, or personalized content to increase engagement and brand awareness.

Where to Find Inspiration: Top Resources for Award-Winning Campaigns

I've always found that studying successful campaigns is one of the best ways to spark new ideas and understand what truly works in marketing. The resources below feature some of my favorite places to explore award-winning campaigns that not only inspire creativity but also drive results. From Cannes Lions to the Effie Awards, these platforms offer great case studies and insights that have shaped how I approach marketing. I hope they inspire you too!

Cannes Lions International Festival of Creativity

Website: www.canneslions.com

Cannes Lions is one of the most prestigious international awards for creative marketing communications. It showcases campaigns that push the boundaries of creativity and effectiveness.

Effie Awards

Website: www.effie.org

The Effie Awards focus on marketing effectiveness. They provide case studies of campaigns that have successfully achieved measurable results and business objectives.

The Shorty Awards

Website: www.shortyawards.com

This award honors the best in social media and digital marketing campaigns. It covers innovative and impactful campaigns across various social media platforms.

The Drum Awards

Website: www.thedrum.com/awards

The Drum Awards celebrate creativity, innovation, and marketing excellence, featuring a variety of categories such as content, digital, and social media campaigns.

Ad Age Creativity Awards

Website: www.adage.com/creativity

Ad Age's Creativity Awards focus on highlighting standout marketing campaigns that demonstrate originality and success.

Webby Awards

Website: www.webbyawards.com

Known for recognizing excellence on the internet, the Webby Awards celebrate digital content, advertising, and marketing that excels in engagement and innovation.

Clio Awards

Website: www.clios.com

The Clio Awards recognize excellence in advertising, design, and communications, with case studies of notable campaigns from around the world.

WARC (World Advertising Research Center)

Website: www.warc.com

WARC provides access to marketing effectiveness insights, reports, and case studies of award-winning campaigns across various sectors.

D&AD (Design and Art Direction) Awards

Website: www.dandad.org

D&AD Awards celebrate creative excellence in design and advertising, offering access to inspirational and effective marketing campaigns.

Marketing Week's Masters of Marketing Awards

Website: www.marketingweek.com

Marketing Week's Masters of Marketing Awards highlight campaigns that have made a significant impact on brand growth and consumer engagement.

CHAPTER 15: INSIGHTS FROM INDUSTRY EXPERTS

Over the course of my career in digital marketing, I've looked to industry leaders who consistently deliver strategies that get results. These experts have shaped the way I think about effective, results-driven marketing—campaigns that don't just look good, but actually work.

While I haven't interviewed them directly for this book, their insights, shared publicly through their work, have had a lasting influence on me.

In this chapter, I've gathered some of their most practical advice to help you build marketing campaigns that truly work—campaigns that convert and drive meaningful outcomes.

Rand Fishkin (Founder of Moz and SparkToro)

Key Insight: Understanding Your Audience for Campaigns that Convert

Rand Fishkin's approach to marketing is rooted in a deep understanding of audience behavior. He emphasizes that successful SEO is not just about keywords—it's about knowing who your audience is, what they're searching for, and how you can deliver content that answers their questions. When you focus on these fundamentals, your campaigns naturally become more effective.

Real-World Example:

A SaaS company implemented Rand's data-driven approach to SEO by analyzing user search patterns and adjusting their content to match specific pain points. This resulted in a significant increase in organic traffic and a measurable boost in conversions, proving that aligning with audience needs delivers results.

Actionable Takeaway:

Invest time in truly understanding your audience's search intent. Use tools like SparkToro or audience research to tailor your SEO strategy for long-term campaign success.

Ann Handley (Chief Content Officer at MarketingProfs)

Key Insight: The Power of Storytelling to Drive Engagement and Action

Ann Handley is a master of using storytelling as a way to make marketing campaigns more relatable and impactful. Her belief is that content should not only inform but inspire action. Campaigns that convert are those that speak to the audience's emotions and experiences, making them feel connected to the brand.

Real-World Example:

An e-commerce brand used Ann's storytelling framework to revamp its email marketing campaigns. Instead of pushing products, they started sharing customer stories and insights. This simple shift increased engagement and led to higher conversion rates, showing the direct impact of storytelling on campaign success.

Actionable Takeaway:

Focus on creating content that resonates emotionally with your audience. Tell stories that reflect their challenges and aspirations, and you'll see a deeper connection that leads to conversions.

Neil Patel (Co-founder of Neil Patel Digital)

Key Insight: Scaling Campaigns that Work through Data and Optimization

Neil Patel's expertise centers on using data to continuously optimize and scale campaigns. Whether it's SEO, content marketing, or paid ads, Neil stresses that the key to success is constant testing and refinement. By optimizing every element of a campaign—headlines, keywords, copy—you can ensure that each piece works harder to convert.

Real-World Example:

A startup working with Neil Patel Digital saw a 35% increase in conversions after adopting Neil's approach to data-driven optimization. By regularly testing different elements of their campaigns, they were able to fine-tune what worked best, scaling their efforts without increasing their ad spend.

Actionable Takeaway:

Embrace data and optimization. Use A/B testing, analytics, and audience feedback to refine your campaigns continuously, ensuring they drive the best possible outcomes.

Gary Vaynerchuk (CEO of VaynerMedia)

Key Insight: Leveraging Social Media for Direct Conversions

Gary Vaynerchuk's strategy focuses on meeting audiences where they are, primarily on social media platforms. His campaigns prioritize building authentic connections through consistent, valuable content. Gary believes that if you're providing genuine value on the platforms where your audience spends their time, conversions will follow.

Real-World Example:

A fashion retailer ran a user-generated content campaign on Instagram and TikTok based on Gary's social media advice. By encouraging customers to share their own photos and experiences with the brand, they increased conversions by 200%, proving that authentic engagement drives action.

Actionable Takeaway:

Leverage social media to build real relationships with your audience. Consistently share valuable, engaging content, and encourage user participation to boost conversions naturally.

Seth Godin (Author and Marketing Thought Leader)

Key Insight: Permission Marketing and Building Trust for Long-Term Success

Seth Godin pioneered the concept of "permission marketing," which focuses on earning your audience's trust by providing value consistently. Campaigns that convert over the long term are built on relationships, not interruptions. Seth's insights remind us that marketing is about building trust over time—earning the right to engage with your audience.

Real-World Example:

A subscription service applied Seth's permission marketing principles by creating a gated content experience for their audience. By offering exclusive, high-value content, they earned the trust of potential customers and saw a significant increase in membership conversions.

Actionable Takeaway:

Focus on creating permission-based campaigns where the audience gives you their attention because they trust you. Offer consistent value in exchange for that attention, and conversions will follow naturally.

Jay Baer (Founder of Convince & Convert)

Key Insight: Enhancing Customer Experience to Drive Repeat Conversions

Jay Baer emphasizes that successful marketing doesn't end at the first conversion—it continues by providing an outstanding customer experience that keeps people coming back. Campaigns that convert repeatedly do so by nurturing relationships and making every customer interaction positive and valuable.

Real-World Example:

A hospitality brand used Jay's advice to revamp its customer service and follow-up email strategy. By personalizing their post-booking communication and offering tailored recommendations, they saw a 15% increase in repeat bookings, proving that a great customer experience can drive long-term conversions.

Actionable Takeaway:

Don't stop after the first sale. Focus on enhancing the post-conversion experience by personalizing interactions, offering support, and nurturing customer relationships to keep conversions coming.

Looking Ahead: Expert Predictions on the Future of Marketing that Works

Each of these experts also has a vision for where marketing is heading, offering forward-thinking insights that can help you stay ahead in the ever-evolving digital landscape:

- **Rand Fishkin:** "SEO will continue to be driven by AI, offering more personalized and precise search experiences. The brands that can keep up with these changes will thrive."
- **Ann Handley:** "Storytelling will become even more crucial in an era where consumers crave authenticity and human connection, especially as AI-generated content becomes more prevalent."
- **Neil Patel:** "Data and automation will drive campaign success, but the ability to personalize marketing based on real-time data will be a key differentiator."
- **Gary Vaynerchuk:** "Short-form video content will dominate, and the ability to create meaningful moments in seconds will separate brands that convert from those that don't."
- **Seth Godin:** "Trust and permission marketing will remain critical as consumers demand more control over their data. Brands that earn trust will have a significant advantage."
- **Jay Baer:** "Customer experience will be a key driver of repeat conversions. Brands that prioritize customer satisfaction and personalization will outperform those that don't."

Expert Advice on Creating and Managing Successful Campaigns

- **Focus on the Customer**: Always keep the customer at the center of your marketing strategy. Understand their pain points, preferences, and behaviors to create more effective campaigns.

- **Embrace Data**: Use data analytics to measure the performance of your campaigns and make informed adjustments. This will help you refine your strategy and improve your ROI.

- **Stay Ahead of Trends**: Keep an eye on emerging trends and be willing to experiment with new technologies and platforms to stay competitive.

Future Trends and Predictions in Digital Marketing

- **AI and Automation**: The integration of AI and automation tools will continue to grow, allowing for more personalized and efficient marketing efforts.

- **Voice Search and Smart Speakers**: As voice search becomes more prevalent, optimizing content for voice queries will be essential.

- **Sustainability and Social Responsibility**: Consumers are increasingly prioritizing brands that demonstrate a commitment to sustainability and social responsibility, making these key areas for future marketing strategies.

CONCLUSION

Recap of Key Plays

As we come to the end, it's important to revisit the key takeaways that will help you build campaigns that deliver results. From setting clear, measurable objectives and deeply understanding your audience, to leveraging data and staying agile in a fast-changing industry, each chapter has provided practical, actionable insights. Whether you're launching your first campaign or optimizing existing strategies, these lessons will empower you to create digital marketing campaigns that drive meaningful and measurable outcomes.

Final Thoughts and Encouragement for Digital Marketers, Entrepreneurs, and Business Owners

Digital marketing is a powerful driver of growth, regardless of your business size or available resources. By applying the strategies and tactics outlined in this book, you have the tools to elevate your brand, meaningfully engage your target audience, and achieve your boldest business goals.

However, success in digital marketing goes beyond mastering tools and techniques—it's about adopting the right mindset. Be open to learning, embrace change, and constantly innovate. Keep experimenting, stay curious, and don't hesitate to pursue bold, creative ideas. Ultimately, it's your willingness to take calculated risks, adapt, and continuously refine your approach that will set you apart, leading to campaigns that don't just look good but actually convert.

ACKNOWLEDGEMENT

I want to extend my deepest gratitude to the small business owners, entrepreneurs, and digital marketers who continue to inspire me with their resilience, creativity, and determination. Your stories, successes, and challenges have been a constant source of motivation in writing this book.

This book is dedicated to all of you. My hope is that it serves as a valuable guide to help you navigate the ever-evolving digital marketing landscape, empowering you to create campaigns that convert and drive your businesses toward even greater success.

ABOUT THE AUTHOR

Sharon Lee Thony

Sharon Lee Thony is a brand and marketing executive with over two decades of experience creating award-winning, results-driven campaigns for travel, beauty, and luxury lifestyle brands. She specializes in crafting marketing strategies that not only elevate brand visibility but also drive tangible business growth.

As the founder and CEO of SLT Consulting, a boutique digital marketing agency, Sharon partners with ambitious businesses, helping them scale through proven marketing strategies that deliver measurable success. Her hands-on approach has made her a trusted advisor for companies looking to optimize their digital marketing efforts and achieve sustainable growth.

Sharon holds a BA from New York University and an MBA from The Wharton School. She delivers keynotes and workshops at industry conferences and has taught over 1,000 classes worldwide as an Adjunct Professor, shaping the next generation of marketers at both undergraduate and graduate institutions.

Made in the USA
Columbia, SC
30 April 2025